Her LOVED Soul

A POETIC JOURNEY THROUGH DATING

By Briana *Ariel*

HER LOVED SOUL
Published in the United States by FREED Publishing

© 2024 by Briana Ariel

ISBN: 979-8-3303-8804-2

Holy Bible: New Living Translation. Wheaton, Ill: Tyndale House Publish-
ers, 2004. Print.

For bookings and all other inquiries www.BrianaAriel.com

A note from the author:

To be transparent is to be exposed. Through a season of self-reflection, I realized I was close to losing love. Not God himself, but in the form of relationships. The brokenness and the pain of getting past previous relationships were driving me to close the door to loving and allowing myself to be truly loved. Fear of being hurt again drove me to begin shutting down the idea of future love.

Even if everything in me wanted to slam the door shut and throw away the key, I couldn't do that. I had to keep the *flame* lit, at least in my mind. With each poem, I fueled the fire. The good, the bad, the past, the present, and the future. I pulled from my experiences and those of the women who support me to give voice to their versions of love. Through this collection of poetry, I discovered pieces of me that revealed my fears, my hopes, and even my shortcomings regarding the way I love others and God.

This is a window into Her Loved Soul.

-Briana *Ariel*

"And do everything with love."
1 Corinthians 16:14 NLT

Acknowledgments
I dedicate this book to *all* of the women whom I
have the pleasure of doing life with. Your friendship,
sisterhood, and vulnerability are unmatched.
I love and cherish you all dearly.

CHAPTER 1

THE ACHES

Promise me, O women of Jerusalem, not to awaken love until the time is right. Young Women of Jerusalem
Song of Solomon 8:4 NLT

|| **her type** ||

if she really wanted you
she would have had you
but you seem all too familiar to her
she has walked with you a few times
allowed you to hype her up
in ways she sorrowfully regretted
invested time in you which yielded
mostly losses
leaving dividends of *lessons*
and even still–
you intrigue her
just like you did the first time

she's encountered your fine stature
her eyes still intrigued by your many
sculptures
you've come in different shades
she has found them all to be appeal-
ing
the dividends left by you taught her
to close her eyes in your presence
so her mind can clearly see through
your slick words and generic affir-
mations
reading between the truth and lies
that you speak so effortlessly

monitoring the inconsistencies of
your movements
she's allowed you to touch her
one time too many
holding her close
whispering the nothings that made
her
hair stand up and her lips quiver
she'd be lying if she said she didn't
consider it
because she *knows* you

what you bring temporarily fixes
the aching of her heart
the longing of her body
and leaves her depleted
five percent satisfaction
ninety-five percent heartache

the dividends of your past encoun-
ters
gave her the courage
to turn off the valves of her heart
barricade the best parts of her
and look to God for strength
to not go around that mountain with
you again
she's officially cutting you off

she's held onto your lies
that you were her only attraction
your height, your smell, your build
always seem to trip her up
claiming she could only be with you
oh the lies she believed her entire
life
dismissing anyone who didn't fit the
mold
she was afraid of not being with you
but being with you was more terri-
fying
than she could have ever imagined
she's serving notice to *her type*
you are officially dethroned

|| **all the feels** ||

sometimes she has the right feelings
in the *wrong season*

|| **all the feels** ||

sometimes she has the right feelings
in the *wrong season*

|| answers ||

God,
i just want to love him
how can I *trust* that he will love me back
when he doesn't love you

the answer:
you can *trust* that he won't

|| equal opportunity sight ||

it doesn't take years to
recognize the light
in someone

equally

it doesn't take years to
recognize the absence of that same light
in someone

|| **out of sync** ||

it seems we are always out of sync
when i want you
you don't want me *equally*
when i walk away
you desire what i once wanted
we continue this pattern of cat and mouse
knowing we should never be in sync
because it's obvious
you are not good for me

|| **facts not truth** ||

the reality of her heart *breaking*
corrupts her mind
into believing this ache will
never go away

|| **cleansing** ||

she detoxed from him
over and over again
until *her blood* no longer
held his chromosomes of poison

|| distant ||

she'd rather love you wholeheartedly
than give you only *glimpses* of her fortified heart
that's why she never returns your calls

|| distant ||

she'd rather love you wholeheartedly
than give you only *glimpses* of her fortified heart
that's why she never returns your calls

|| nonsymmetrical paths ||

we are in two different spaces
running two different races
moving at *unparalleled paces*

|| one track mind ||

wishing he was more interested in
caressing her mind
than caressing her thighs
his constant attempts
are reminders of why
he is not *equipped* to be with her
so she let him stay on that track
alone

|| wavering ||

she didn't know how strong her own will was
until she was led to walk away
from someone she loved
the decision to separate herself from him
was obviously the right choice

but her will
that she thought was surrendered to God completely
kept her in the doorway between
her heart and her head

stuck.

wavering.

between what's best for her
and what she wanted in that moment

|| **deflector** ||

in hindsight
she sees
he ferociously pointed out
everyone else's flaws
to keep her from *seeing* his

|| **deflector** ||

in hindsight
she sees
he ferociously pointed out
everyone else's flaws
to keep her from *seeing* his

|| **her first love** ||

she used to love him
even into her adulthood
thoughts of him still lingered
young love is as reckless
as an uncontrolled fire
smoldering long after its extinction

she used to love him
late-night conversations
gift exchanges
they deposited much more
friends and lovers
too young to understand the depths

she used to love him
too naïve to understand
wasn't mature enough
didn't know enough
wasn't *whole enough*
at the time
to explore the attraction

she used to love him
or so she thought it was love
except she didn't know how
to truly give what she didn't have
and he didn't know either
so they exchanged their best
and worst features
trying to pour out pure love
from a dirty hose

|| unequally yoked ||

her light quietly dimmed
as she poured her energy
into the empty well of him
she *yoked* her mind with his
dimming the shine
that initially attracted him to her

|| **desperation** ||

in her most desperate state
where loneliness and failure
tries to overshadow her truth

i hope she runs to you, Lord
where you will fill her with
the *intimate* love
she is so desperate for

‖ tight squeeze ‖

she tried to make him fit into her world
ignoring the obvious
squinting at the imperfections in *his character*
she fought the uneasy confirmation
that he, indeed, is not God's best

‖ tight squeeze ‖

she tried to make him fit into her world
ignoring the obvious
squinting at the imperfections in *his character*
she fought the uneasy confirmation
that he, indeed, is not God's best

|| **superhuman woman** ||

she over-extended herself enough
to recognize she's not superhuman
even if she feels like she can be *all* things to *all* people
in her soul, she knows it's not true
and yet she still continues to say yes
while she runs on fumes

|| **superhuman woman** ||

she over-extended herself enough
to recognize she's not superhuman
even if she feels like she can be *all* things to *all* people
in her soul, she knows it's not true
and yet she still continues to say yes
while she runs on fumes

|| **too** ||

we're too much
way too much
too much
in two different directions
two opposites
two foundations
of opposition
too convicted of our truths
to compromise
two souls
not predestined to be
less than two

|| rejected heart ||

she took his rejection
swallowed her pride
and allowed God to interpret the pain

God showed her
she was *worth loving*
however
the man she loved
didn't have the capacity
to love her

so he discarded her
out of his *own* insecurities

she accepted the truth
but the pain
still lingered

|| **divorced** ||

a three-stranded cord is not easily broken
but somehow, he intently *unraveled himself* from their union
with the same amount of tenacity
he used to weave them together

|| **divorced** ||

a three-stranded cord is not easily broken
but somehow, he intently *unraveled himself* from their union
with the same amount of tenacity
he used to weave them together

|| **heartaches** ||

when your heart bursts
the initial explosion
is followed by
many micro-explosions
going off
one
after another
as your brain tries to
console the uneasiness of your soul
the pain, *at times* unbearable
needs more than ice cream
and a shopping spree
this is an ache
only Jesus can fix

|| another project ||

she finally learned to identify him for who he was
not for who she knew he could be
she originally labeled him as a potential partner
wisdom and *time* revealed he was simply a project
not suitable for a lifetime

|| another project ||

she finally learned to identify him for who he was
not for who she knew he could be
she originally labeled him as a potential partner
wisdom and *time* revealed he was simply a project
not suitable for a lifetime

|| cheater ||

i've cheated on you
time and time again

ignoring your knocks
drowning out your whispers

i've clung to seasons you
wanted me to let go of

i've climbed mountains
for some who didn't deserve
my level of love
while leaving you
standing
knocking
waiting
to have all of me

your stance compelled me
to lay down my cheating ways

i give in
to your advances
and give you all of me

forgive me, heavenly father

|| say it ain't so ||

she wanted to be in love
she desired it *wholeheartedly*
without reason she
wholeheartedly accepted the closest version
of semi-good love that approached her
she knew better
but even in all her knowledge
she temporarily accepted less than God's best

|| self-reflection ||

sometimes
she too
is reminded
of her own
shortcomings
in the way
she loves

|| ghost 'em ||

she learned that every text doesn't need a response
life won't stop if she ignores his call
guarding her heart is a lot simpler
once she cut off *the signal* to him

|| ghost 'em ||

she learned that every text doesn't need a response
life won't stop if she ignores his call
guarding her heart is a lot simpler
once she cut off *the signal* to him

|| known fact ||

abuse of any kind
is *not* love

32

|| rip tides of love ||

i've come to the obvious conclusion
that we are on two different waves
every time i try to get close to you
i'm swept away by the current

the opposing forces of our lives
are like riptides
dragging me further and further
away from you

high tide arrived tonight
and in that moment i wanted you close
i reached out wanting to anchor
pieces of my truth in you

but you didn't answer the call
as i rode the rip current once again
i realized i will *never win* swimming against
the natural flow of my own wave

|| empty promises ||

the empty promises
he feeds her
have left her malnourished
she's starving for *consistency*
for real honest answers

his empty promises
made her heart growl in anguish
getting let down by him
week after week
was actually the perfect setup
for her hungry heart
to take a seat at *someone else's* table

|| **hindsight 20/20** ||

she'd mistaken acts of good character as a sign of a changed life
not knowing at the time
that anyone can put makeup on a broken heart
hiding the emptiness in works
she missed the signs
she learned to ask God to reveal others' hearts
she learned not to trust in what she sees
but to trust in the one
who *sees her fully*

|| these legal papers ||

she wondered how she would feel
as the day grew closer
to legally being free
would she cry
would she be full of joy
would she lose her mind

the papers are in her hand
as she reviews every word
she sees the possibility of what could have been
and reminisces on the pain that was
it wasn't always bad
there were laughs, sweet words, fun adventures
but the crash at the end almost took her out
breathless
soaked in her tears
her heart had so many bullet wounds

she has forgiven
her heart is healed
as she holds these papers
she feels peace
a heart full of gratitude
that she fought until she heard God say enough
she didn't throw in the towel without a fight

|| **incapable** ||

she has loved you enough to know
that you cannot love her
with *equal* or *greater* depth
on your best day
she is still oozing
in desire for the one thing
you are incapable of giving her

|| ego soother ||

she downplayed her achievements
to massage his ego
she outwardly diminished her worth
in a *hopeless* effort to maintain his

|| seeing the horizon ||

she flirts with temptation
this time she sees it clearly
planning her way of escape
strategically resisting her norms
certain this time she will be *victorious*

|| teenage infatuation ||

at 19, a rush from your spine
feels like love that will never end

she made permanent decisions
on a *temporary sensation*

youthful infatuation
transformed into wisdom

as she retraces the miscalculated steps
that brought her here

|| **sabbatical** ||

the distance gives her
clarity
to
see you for who you *really* are
and how *distant* you are
from who she needs you to be

|| **misappropriation** ||

she aspired to be
nothing more than
the apple of someone's eyes
her misappropriated values
left her wanting heart
void of her *true worth*

|| temptation calls ||

Jesus did not lay His life down
for me to put myself back into the *chains of sin*

|| sight hound ||

she wonders why
she's *only relevant*
when she's in your sight
stroking your ego with her presence
and poof
you disappear again
as the days go on

|| potential isn't enough ||

when she realized
that she couldn't change him
and had to accept him
for who he currently is
and let go of his potential
he lost all of his appeal

|| all the signs ||

every step forward in his direction
is *always* met with a detour
a failure in communication
conflicting schedules
electronic malfunctions
she's starting to think
there's a reason
she is being *shielded* from him

|| **moody** ||

her unstable emotions
are a reflection
of his *unstable heart*

47

|| misinterpretation ||

was it *really* love
or simply a human attempt
to fulfill the need
that had swelled within her being
so long that even with its fallacies
she considered what it was
to at one point have been real

|| **toll road of love** ||

let the record show
the first bloom of love in her heart for you
was in your brokenness
at your weakest point
she *chose* to open a fraction of her heart to yours

at your lowest, she felt you grow distant
she reached out to let you know her heart was stirred
but the confusion of your instability
spilled over into her head and she became unsure

so *she retreated*
closing the door because at your lowest
she knew you could take a toll on her
that she could not afford even if her
heart desperately wanted to

|| heartbreak on the horizon ||

what happens when what she needs
isn't what she wants

and when what she wants
is all she *thinks* she needs

|| good guy, wrong season ||

she wanted to know him
to understand him
yet his schedule
full to the brim
left little time for her to listen to his heart
she knew even if he penciled her in
it wouldn't be *enough*
to answer all of the questions
billowing inside her heart

|| butterfly-less ||

she knows love is not a feeling
yet she questions the present
wanting to explore him
knowing she could if she tried
but void of the usual butterflies
she's always *assumed* to accompany love
without the emotional roller coaster
of highs, lows, and head-over-heels attraction
she's not sure what to call it

|| sacrifice ||

i wept as i watched her
abort the dreams
that she carried
nurtured and loved
because she knew
she couldn't *birth* her baby
and his at the same time

|| impatient and bored ||

she cheats on her future with *her present*
knowing the consequences
of impatience
and even still
she *entertains him*

|| so i entertain ||

what i want from you
i know you can't give
i entertain the conversation
because i'm intrigued
by our communication
my mind likes the stimulation
little *glimpses* of intimacy
even in theory i still enjoy

knowing you will never satisfy me
i wonder *why i keep you*
close enough to expose pieces of me
far enough to protect my body
from being your next victim

i love the thought of you
because it reminds me of a season
i dwelled in for so long
i enjoy the game and play it strategically
because i know i love myself too much
to gift myself to you *wholeheartedly*
you aren't deserving of all that i am
so i settle for conversations
about fictitious scenarios about us
that *my soul* knows will never come true

|| **life lessons** ||

she detached herself
from the possibility of ever being his
because she couldn't bear the rejection

she knew
he was only curious
but wasn't invested

thoughts of him lingered
until she realized her fantasy and his reality
were *worlds apart*
she began to resist the thought
until she emptied herself of the desire
for a man who could never satisfy the longing of her soul

|| "frie-lationship" ||

with a heavy heart
she broke up with a man
she wasn't even officially with
to her dismay
the tearing felt *equally* as hard
as the *real* thing

|| impatience ||

she temporarily bought into *the lie*
that she would never find her true soul mate

so she settled for imitation after imitation
slowly each one sucked her dry

she finally believed
that one day she would meet the one she could envision her life with
and when that day came
she wanted to have something left to offer

so *by faith* she stopped giving out her samples
and depleting her reserves with fillers

|| the tie ||

she sees it crystal clear
the fruit of his tree can be bitter some days
even her friends warn her to *tread lightly*
she steps cautiously closer to him
she embraces his empty hugs
then pulls away
because *even her body knows*
he doesn't fit the mold
and still, she entertains fragments of him

|| played ||

how did she wind up
holding the pieces of her mangled heart in her hands
figuring out how to *rewire* her brain
to stop hurting
she believed the lies he spoke so eloquently
running circles around her
as he played his melody of game
she fell
hard
like an egg
she cracked
oozing out her yoke
only to be left to pick up her shell *alone*

|| her motives ||

does she love him
or just the *thought* of him

does she lust for him
or truly want to merge her spirit with him

does she want company
or true companionship with him

does she want a true friendship
or just another man *affirming* her worth

|| netflix & chill ||

she thought she could deposit her heart
time and time again
exchanging small fragments for
love, affection, and good conversation
she treated her heart like her netflix account
everyone had the password

they monitored her heart when *convenient*

she allowed it
because the streaming made her feel loved
even if it was temporary
she learned to accept
the diminished returns
until even the scraps were not enough

so she changed her password

|| **level up** ||

i want character but i have yet to see
the level that i need
to entrust my soul to yours
so with a heavy heart
i pass on every opportunity
to *solidify my life* with yours

|| bad choice ||

she awakened something
she was not completely ready for
now she struggles to carry the weight
of her *awakening*

|| gasping ||

conversations with him give me a hit
of *temporary* satisfaction
but never truly fulfill my craving

our exchanges leave me gasping for more
even if i overdosed on him
i'd still have a huge hole
that *only God* can fill

|| empty desires ||

what's broken in her?
there has to be a reason
she keeps wanting to keep him close
knowing he's not good for her

|| **weighted** ||

loving you
isn't as easy as i thought loving you would be
the bags on bags of baggage
weigh me down daily
having to *overextend* my heart
for the unnecessary loads you brought
is *exhausting*

|| struggle for freedom ||

she would have chosen him over a million bucks
packed with opportunity and romantic illusions
she knew that the world would crash and still he would cling to her
she painted a collage of them
in her mind on her heart and in her soul
making it *impossible* to walk away
even when she had every reason to let go

|| samples of her ||

she allowed him to touch pieces of her
well before he completed his purchase
she willingly gave out *samples*
reminding him of what he could one day fully have

she undervalued her worth
thinking that if she withheld
he would abort the mission
even with generous deposits of self
the *inevitable* was bound to happen

and this cycle repeated itself time and time again

|| choosing a king ||

"Better to hear the quiet words of a wise person than the shouts of a foolish
king."
Ecclesiastes 9:17 NLT

i hear him calling me
barking in boldness
he addresses me with strength
but i *recognize the dog in him*
he is definitely a king in his own right
chiseled from good stock
if only fool wasn't his middle name
i'd allow myself to serve him
without reservations
i would accept his proposal
to be his queen
today i *declined*
because i prefer *quiet words* of wisdom from a wise man
over the shouts of a foolish king

|| **just an option** ||

if he wanted her to be the only option
he would make that known
otherwise she wouldn't feel like
she jumps from 1st to 3rd
depending on how the *wind blows*

|| fabricated love ||

and just like that
he consistently shows her
how inconsistent his love and affection truly is
pulling away just as quickly as he clung to her
sending empty text messages
to let her know he still sees her
even from
afar

|| mr. intellectual ||

his intelligence
as intriguing as it is
is the *one thing*
that gets in the way
of the true love of his soul
he has too much knowledge
not enough wisdom
for her to submit her life to his

|| **shipwrecked** ||

i love you enough to let you go
i love you enough to take control
of this wild train we've been riding on
skipping tracks like a scratched cd
we've just been *depleting* each other

every bump in the road made us weaker not stronger
i can no longer stay and drift like the wind
into the ocean of this reckless relationship
i'm choosing to save both of us
by walking away from our destructive shipwreck

|| **vulture** ||

he hooked her once again
his claws sunk deep
piercing her heart
she was free
but she chose to go back into his enclosure
ignoring the danger sign

|| the empty condo ||

as i sit here in this empty space
i think of an empty vase
full of our future, shattered
glass all around cluttering my mind
as i realize those hopes are gone

the empty space reminds me of my empty heart
i've made time to clear it out
the crevices that held your voice
and the stretch marks that our destruction left
are being filled and repaired daily

i feast on the word of God
until His voice evicts the pain that tries to make its home in me
i speak words by faith to fight the broken words that replay in my mind
i let this empty space be filled with the greatest of all time
as i unwind the past years and expose my fears
He takes the tears and bottles each of them

pouring *His joy* out on my broken bones
even they cry out for God's love
reminding me i'm not as broken as i once was
and even though you left
i've never not been loved

CHAPTER 2
REFLECTIONS OF SELF

RESTORATION, WHOLENESS, AND A WHOLE LOT OF JESUS.

Now we see things imperfectly, like puzzling reflections in a mirror, but then we will see everything with perfect clarity. All that I know is partial and incomplete, but then I will know everything completely, just as God now knows me completely.
1 Corinthians 13:12 (NLT)

|| if only i knew to love me ||

if only i knew
how badly you desperately needed
to know the truth

if only i knew
i would have started loving you *sooner*
investing my time
depositing words of affirmation
into your soul
guarding you from the lies
building you up from the inside out
then you wouldn't have to rely
on the words of someone else

if only i knew
to love myself

i could have started
thriving long ago

|| armored ||

she gathered the beating parts of her heart
fortified it with a hard outer shell
the chains wrapped around it so tight
that they left permanent indents
feeling emotionless
she lived recklessly
thinking that every encounter
meant absolutely nothing
in reality each encounter
worked its way into her shell
leaving small gashes in her armor
reacting out of anger
when she was hurt
thinking it was her protection
but it was just the *evidence*
that she wasn't as secure as she originally thought

|| the process ||

she temporarily detached her heart
to *solely* give it to Jesus
for his healing
in the solitude of his love
he prepared her to have the courage
to reattach her heart
to love *after* being broken

|| **wholeness** ||

i am too whole
to *settle* for only fragments of you

|| **wholeness** ||

i am too whole
to *settle* for only fragments of you

|| cycles ||

i've lived with myself long enough
to identify the cyclical
tendencies of my heart
so i leave *markers*
reminding me to jump off the wheel
not wanting to repeat that lesson again

|| cycles ||

i've lived with myself long enough
to identify the cyclical
tendencies of my heart
so i leave *markers*
reminding me to jump off the wheel

|| **her needs** ||

a strong woman
still desires a place
to lay her head
and *her heart*

|| **heart check** ||

i've challenged my heart
not to love everything it *sees*
not to believe everything it feels
and not to trust all of the words it *hears*
the heart is deceitful
who can truly know its hidden truths
but God

|| her emotional wave ||

she doesn't want to be in her feelings
experiencing all the percolations of her fears and her heart being torn
yet understanding that in order to get to the shore
she has to ride this wave fully
wanting to hitch a ride on a boat
to ignore the waves of her *feelings*
yet knowing every rip of the tide must be felt
facing the storm head-on
will get her to the shores of peace *quicker*

|| her raw materials ||

i need you to love the raw materials
i'm warning you there are pieces of me
that even *i am uneasy* with
yet i unapologetically choose to love me
because i know they won't always be there
they are tender and moldable
i'm willing to bend and twist into the best version of me
are you willing to love me
in my *rawest form*
as an abstract piece of art

|| guarding her life ||

she loves herself *enough*
to be her own advocate
set her own standard
accept the good
and *reject* who and what
does not give her peace

|| her journey to wholeness ||

there was a time in her life
where she lived out of her suitcase
running from city to city
event to event
calling it *purpose*
and yes each venue had some ounce of truth
however she knew at her core
she needed a distraction
from her present situation

one day she chose to stop
just for a season
to clear out the cobwebs of her life
let go of her toxic relationship
allow God to *breathe life* into her again
decompress from the abuse she left
it was time for her to get whole
and whole *she became*

|| **sooner** ||

sooner or later
she's going to have to face her fears
and open herself to love again

she needs *more faith*
than ever before
to love

|| his true nature ||

how can you express love
without knowing love
without engaging in conversations with him
it's utterly impossible
he is love
in all ways
he exhibits
his true nature

|| spring dreams ||

letdowns
come
their pain
at times lingers
like the coldest of winters

but *keep hope* in your heart
because spring always comes
sometimes later than expected
but nevertheless
you will bloom again

|| a lovely legacy ||

one day she will love unapologetically
caress her words with grace
her partnership will build a legacy
generations will *stand* on her covenant
she holds on to this hope
because she knows the greatness that dwells beneath her core
is simultaneously moving toward the greatness that dwells beneath his
the collision of two souls who belong to the *same king*
creating royalty in their union
they will fulfill their destiny

|| no filter ||

can you appreciate
the art that i am
even with the flawed strokes
can you *still* find the beauty *within me*

|| no filter ||

can you appreciate
the art that i am
even with the flawed strokes
can you *still* find the beauty *within me*

|| the never-ending search ||

she's looking for a savior
when she already has one
no wonder her *wandering heart*
is constantly disappointed

|| **sunrise** ||

love is on the horizon
i see it *rising* in my heart
kissing the dark clouds away

|| redirecting my energy ||

i've given too much energy
to empty romances
slow dances
kisses of *fruitless sensations*
leaving me
senseless
wondering, is it love?
knowing it's only lust
and the *illusion* of what
my heart so desperately
longs to experience

the desire
exploits my brain's ability
to decipher between
authentic love
and its alluring illusion
i need more than its temporary highs
and earth-shattering lows
i need a constant love
even with the ebbs
and flows
by my side
holding my heart
breathing life into me
when doubt tries to take root

the kind of love where
intellect
spirit
and emotion connect
producing a *covenant*
sealed with a sexual pleasure
undefiled in every way
culminating its authenticity daily
this is what i'm in need of

i'm saving my newfound
energy on what is *real*

|| first and foremost ||

i want to love you more than anything
more than my desire for a mate
more than the expansion of my bank account
more than the cars, jewelry, and clothes
more than the dreams that keep me up at night
more than *everything and all things*
Jesus, i want to love you *first*

|| space to heal ||

she took the time needed
to be alone
without distractions
just her
to feel
to *release*
to break free of her previous relationship
no clutter
just reflection
a few tears
formed new wisdom
that she will tote with her
as she prepares her heart
to be *held once again*

|| her single heart ||

she prayed until
her heart was content
in its present state
in that moment
single and *whole*

|| her single heart ||

she prayed until
her heart was content
in its present state
in that moment
single and *whole*

|| despacio ||

she's rushed through this
over and over
checking the box
seeking perfection

with time comes wisdom
she knows now
that perfection is found
in an *imperfect journey*

she slows her pace
enough to inhale
welcoming love with every breath
she's enjoying the journey

|| **her standard** ||

if God's not in him
then i don't want him

if he doesn't *submit* to God
then i don't want to submit to him

if God's not in it
then i don't want it

|| my heart's plea ||

Jesus
can you awaken my heart
it's frozen
ice cold
due to the failed attempt
of my last relationship

i'm scared

the *thought of love*
makes my knees shake
and my heart tremble
because i know the vulnerability it takes
to allow someone to get close

even in the intimacy of conversation
i'm afraid of being hurt
of being abandoned
of giving myself to someone
who is unwilling or incapable
of giving back
unconditional love to me

|| **miss** ||

as she stretches
her legs and arms extended across her bed
she sees the beauty in this season
there will be a time for cuddles
and selfless exchanges of self with her future spouse
but now is a time for her
to love herself
because even in her singleness
she lacks no good thing

|| the right prescription ||

like a physician, we must evaluate ourselves
to determine what medication we need
when our *feelings* get us out of whack

|| grace in love ||

will she slow down *enough*
to allow love to take its natural course
entering into her presence
not rushing the ebbs and flows of the emotions
but graciously welcoming the companionship of another

|| grace in love ||

will she slow down *enough*
to allow love to take its natural course
entering into her presence
not rushing the ebbs and flows of the emotions
but graciously welcoming the companionship of another

|| the shift ||

at some point
along the journey
she decided to stop auditioning for roles

she always presented herself in a way
to be placed on a special mantle
in a man's heart

at some point, *she shifted*
knowing she didn't want to be always perfectly poised
or boxed into whatever constraint he desired in a woman

she took off her mask
and the real authentic version of herself surfaced
sometimes poised, others unrefined

she knew she was special in many ways
and only a *certain breed*
could truly embrace all that she is

|| inspect-her gadget ||

she inspected her heart
every crevice of its thinking
sometimes idiotically spending
too much time focused on
failed attempts of love
she kept inspecting
drawing patterns of misuses
identifying the longing
the desire that made her stumble
she left inscriptions as she inspected
leaving reminders
of *worth*
acceptance
and *love*

|| imprinted soul ||

she is loved
even in her brokenness
she *gives love*
pain can't take root
where God's light
has already been imprinted on *her soul*

|| **provision** ||

she has no need
that the Lord has not met
his provision is far beyond
her realm

|| her journal pages ||

some things are better left unsaid
so she writes them in her journal
to give them an *escape* from her mind
freeing her lips from saying truths
that should *never* be spoken

some things are better left unsaid
so she writes them in her journal
to give them an *escape* from her mind
freeing her lips from saying truths
that should *never* be spoken

|| ex-control freak ||

i want to hold you close
not in a romantic sense
but in a possessive one

i want to cling so tight to you
not because i love you
but because i'm scared
of what may actually happen
if i let you be free

so i want to cling to you
suffocating us in the process
gripped by fear

so before saying yes to you
i say no to me
no to owning you as my *personal possession*
or regulating every aspect of your life
i'll play my role
and *release control* to allow
God to play his in your life

|| faithful ||

shout out to the ones who stayed close
who never wavered
the ones who said they loved me
and followed their words with actions
the distance of others made me distrust them
but for those
the ones that stayed close
your authenticity
confirmed that your word
is your word
and your love *doesn't* change
based on either of our present circumstances

thank you.

|| her first love ||

she fell in love with Jesus, ***first.***
that's why it was so easy for her to walk away
when the way you attempted to love her
felt foreign from the love she experienced daily
with her *first love*

|| self-love ||

she could love anyone in the world
yet she *chooses* to love you
even with all your imperfections
and she knows them all
she chooses you

|| **her unapologetic love** ||

her healed heart
birthed the miraculous

daily she loves
as unconditional as possible
knowing that only God
could have breathed life back into
the deepest gash
she ever experienced

in her gratitude
she loves *unapologetically*

|| it's time ||

she's so ready to be organically in love
in *preparation* by faith
she began to snip the dead ends
off of her present love life
fall deeper in love with herself
and head over heels in love with her creator

|| the deceleration ||

i've chosen to place my heart in reserve
for the man who will *enrich my soul* with his presence
i refuse to allow bystanders glimpses
and tastes of my being
because i know my future self would regret my negligence

i will *dwell in purpose* as i wait
building up my faith, my businesses, and my relationships
knowing i am whole even before he enters my world
reassures me that i don't have to entertain foolery in my wait
i'm alone by choice because i have the strength and self-control
to wait for *God's best* for my life

|| resilient woman ||

don't let her smile fool you
she's weathered some of the
toughest storms
and still has a heart full of love to give

|| authentic love ||

somewhere along the road
she started to fall in love with the authentic version of herself
a love affair *so rare*
she cherishes it with all that she is

|| embrace the season ||

just keep living sweetheart
what's for you
will always be for you

no need to slow your pace
embrace this season
paint it with your beauty

hold your chin high
and keep your *standards higher*
the best is yet to come

|| **maturity** ||

she settled for a carbon copy
of the man she once wanted
only to realize she is in a new space
with a deeper mind
and more wisdom
as she *evolves* as a woman
the levels of her being expand
making it easier to weed out
the men who don't fit the mold

|| freed from soul ties ||

thank you for removing the *taste* of his lips from mine
and discarding his empty words from my heart
it's taken me years to rid my sheets of his scent
i finally feel the release of that soul tie

|| **lovely reminder** ||

i'd rather love all of me
the fragmented pieces
are beautiful reminders of my story
the physical and emotional scars
some arrived by accident
and some intentional mishaps
they too are reminders
of how an imperfect person
can be deeply loved
by an all-knowing
unchanging
forgiving
God

|| **desires** ||

the desires
they pull me away
my escape
lost in the allure
fantasizing of what could be
seeing the pattern
over and over again
a warning flag of caution
determining if my desires are his
the ones that aren't always crash and burn
leaving my heart scorched
and my mind drained
having to once again recover
from another episode of my own show
where i *write* the script
as if i am omniscient

i desire his desires
i throw mine into the fire
daily they return
plaguing my thoughts
so i burn them
over and over again
until all that's left is *his*

|| wreck ||

she crashed
into him
trying to *temporarily*
fill a void
larger than the ocean
deeper than the valley
hoping that affection
would begin to make whole
what has been barren
for what seemed like a lifetime
so she crashed
over and over
not realizing
she needed
a savior
Jesus

|| **his aroma** ||

she saviors his scent
because she doesn't know
when he will visit her
in that way again
Jesus

|| the secret cure ||

the more she prayed
the less she desired
to spend her time
with empty words
and *fruitless* exchanges with him

|| unraveled ||

i allowed his love to unravel me to my core
knowing i wouldn't be the same

i embrace the process daily
because i trust God *wholeheartedly*

|| **her forever love** ||

you see me clearly
and even still
you are madly in love with me
how *undeserving*
and incredibly grateful
i am to be loved
and fully known
by you

|| this seat is taken ||

if he can't *feed* your soul
stop giving him a seat at your table
and allowing him to *eat* your fruit

|| love will find you ||

i'm sure you wonder
why love hasn't visited your door
there's *nothing* wrong with your smile
you radiate every room you walk into
don't be discouraged
keep *discovering* the secrets of you
to present your best self
when love comes knocking at your door

|| little tornado ||

she can be a tornado of love
and a hurricane of fear
tossing back and forth with her emotions
she *redirects* her fear into *faith*
daily so she can shield you from
the painful lessons she's learned
throughout her journey to freedom

|| **lookout** ||

don't miss the miracles
that *revolutionize* the storm
bring light to darkness
love in barrenness

|| shortcomings ||

i could love you
all of you
if only i *knew* how to love
for now i can only offer the best parts of me
hoping they will outshine the brokenness under the surface

|| shortcomings ||

i could love you
all of you
if only i *knew* how to love
for now i can only offer the best parts of me
hoping they will outshine the brokenness under the surface

|| Him – Jesus ||

he told me he wanted to love me back to life
so i let him

giving him access to every inch of me
he dug and exposed the fragmented pieces

restoring the parts of me that i allowed others to take freely
not knowing they could never return it in its *entirety*

|| him – my man ||

will he be strong enough to *face* my past
and gentle enough to *love* me in my present
smart enough to *see* through my exterior
and wise enough to *seek* God before seeking me

|| unveiled ||

i'm not accustomed to being vulnerable
being real comes as natural as the wind blows
but even all my realness is still *void of vulnerabilities*

being vulnerable is like walking on foreign soil to me
with every step i'm practicing the language
of this new-found territory with you

and still i'm working overtime
to keep up some walls
that have given me a sense of security for so long

however if i am truly honest and vulnerable...

the peace of your arrival
ushered you
right past the barbed wire fence i installed
and into a space that only God could have prepared in my heart

i'm mustering up the *courage* to push past my fears
and open my heart to yours

i'm audaciously trusting God
to be completely vulnerable with you

CHAPTER 3
LOVE IS ON THE HORIZON

He has made everything beautiful in its time.
Ecclesiastes 3:11 NLT

|| preparation ||

dear future sir
i am loving you
even at a distance
i am loving you *wholeheartedly*
by loving God and myself first
i am creating a safe place for you
a place where my words don't cut
and my eyes are fixated on yours alone
to be in a position where my ears attentively listen to your voice
i am preparing to store your deepest emotions
and support your larger-than-life dreams
i'm *cultivating* an environment
of honesty and transparency
so that i will love you without reservations

|| free falling ||

this time she refuses to force love
she gave up trying to *orchestrate fate*
the symphonies from her past
are reminders of why she no longer meddles

this time she's surrendering to God's perfect plan
she's seen firsthand how he turns ashes into beauty
so she hands over the ashes of her life
knowing her heavenly father will make it beautiful

|| the spark ||

she had almost forgotten what it felt like to be held
to be in the arms of a man
who restrained his strength to *gently* pull her close
in so many ways it felt as if she was gifted another chance to love

|| the art of love ||

we'd paint the sky purple
if only our love had the ability to do so
expressing the colors of our hearts
two rainbows colliding
creating an array of beauty
reflecting *Jesus's* unfailing love

|| exploration of the soul ||

the raw *unfiltered* version of us
exchanges of self
are becoming more frequent
the intimacy in our conversation
exhilarates beyond the vibrations of our words
we are allowing each other
a glimpse into our souls
as we unearth whether we are the perfect match

|| the war to love again ||

i war with the idea of never grasping you again
never pulling you close
when you are here in my grasp, I sometimes feel uneasy
knowing that it's possible to not have you here *always*

i wrestle with the idea of being held
what will happen if the expression of you leaves again
i want to hold you and share you with another
every time i've had you it's always been a battle
the last one *almost* took me out

still i want to hold you again
in your rawest form
without restraint
i want to hold
love

|| standing at the door ||

i'm scared to let you love me
to open myself to you
to the *possibility*
of holding you close
too close
i want to let you in
i haven't figured out just how yet

|| my heart's desire ||

i want an *uncommon* kind of love
with a little common
poetic justice
romantic evenings
no need to spend money
lay and look at the stars

not asking for a lot
but *character* is expensive
i realize i'm not most women
more impressed by his mind
than the clothes he wears
i care more about *his prayers*
his thoughts and his dreams

i carry my own
so i'm looking for a leader
a teacher, a servant
the uncommon type of common
someone i can grow with
a laugh and explore type of creature

the one who looks to God to see me
that's that uncommon type of man
that's the kind of love i want to see

|| **radiate** ||

light recognizes light
you *attracted* me from hundreds of miles away
your flame radiates daily

HER LOVED SOUL | Briana *Ariel*

|| **radiate** ||

light recognizes light
you *attracted* me from hundreds of miles away
your flame radiates daily

147

|| who are you? ||

are you *safe* for my soul
can i grow with you
were we cut from the same cloth

|| to be seen by you ||

when your eyelids
gently kiss your face
i hope your pupils
still keep me in *focus*

i hope my presence
never escapes your sight
even when we are
miles apart

i hope you *train* your eyes
to see me clearly
beyond the depths of my skin

in the darkness of temptation
i hope you still see my light
and cling to its magnetic force

to be seen without being seen
that's a supernatural sight
i hope we see

|| courageous woman ||

last time she let her heart lead
this time she acknowledged its reception of him and *waited*
patiently to allow the cobwebs of newfound love to dissipate

she questioned everything
knowing how tumultuous
a huge miscalculated decision would be

last time she received approval from everyone
however, this time
she *only* seeks the approval of God

so she approached God
over and over again
until clarity and peace blessed her
with the courage, even while scared
to say yes to loving him

|| the way she loves ||

if for whatever reason her heart stopped beating
she hopes the way she loved you
would keep her *alive* in your heart
forever

|| the way she loves ||

if for whatever reason her heart stopped beating
she hopes the way she loved you
would keep her *alive* in your heart
forever

|| aspiration to love ||

i aspire to touch your soul
with open arms, i will receive your truth
allowing our journey to *break* the fears
that have created cobwebs
in my most sacred spaces
i'm *opening* myself to love
and to unapologetically be loved

|| **no resistance** ||

how can she resist the king in you?
your *gravitational pull*
compels her in ways
she has never encountered before

pushing past her fears
to explore the very essence of your being
finding beauty even in your flaws
she's enamored with your design

empowered by your *character*
how can she act as if you are not exotic
she stands before you
admiring the rare breed that you are

praising God for his workmanship
she sees where your flawed past
met God's grace and mercy
how can she resist the king in you?

|| soundtrack ||

let's create a soundtrack of
love and grace
place our hearts on the record
and allow God to spin our love forever
on repeat daily
allowing the harmony of life's ebbs and flows
to serenade this world with a *reflection* of God's love

|| harmonic love ||

loving you is beautiful
the reflection of your presence
on the window frame of my heart
melts my soul
from the inside out

in a puddle of our union
i allow you to dwell within secret places of me
holding me close
our skin blends as one
creating an even tone
of harmony

as butterflies explore one another's untold truths
hidden gems of your words
massage their way into my ears
vocalizing our fears
vowing to stay still
in this moment forever

as the waves toss
wrapped in thick ropes
we anchor ourselves
to *Jesus*
allowing him to calm the sea
within our union

|| honest observations ||

in the silence
you know you're ready
to open up
once again
to *giving*
and
receiving
love

|| her soul ||

he captured her spirit
before she opened the door to her
mind.
will.
and emotions.

|| his eyes ||

when i look into your eyes
i see my reflection
you pierce right through my tough exterior
ripping down the walls i hold up with my fears

in a split second
i'm exposed
in my vulnerability

you point out what others can't see
and your *sincere words*
transform me into a
better version of myself

|| **enamored** ||

admiration of his passions
she's intrigued
eyes wide open
heart still *fully* protected
she watches
searching for the drive
that fuels him
she asks questions
this is rare for her
but she is too *enamored*
to resist
she admires him
wondering if he is
just as enamored
as she is

|| the quintessential question ||

at my core
do i find peace in *uniting*
myself with him

this question
keeps me up at night

|| the quintessential question ||

at my core
do i find peace in *uniting*
myself with him

this question
keeps me up at night

|| kingdom man ||

once she saw the king in him
she couldn't resist exploring his realm of life
intrigued by his intellect and impressed by *his character*
she knew before he even spoke he was fit to *potentially* lead her for life

|| equations ||

make your home in my heart
i'm welcoming you in
opening the floodgates
to you and *only you*
because God chose you
before i even recognized
that you were the perfect addition to my equation

|| the rumble of his joy ||

his laugh
oh his laugh
ignites suddenly
into a roar of *deep joy*
oh his laugh
how beautiful and contagious
it brings smiles to even the most *callous* of hearts
oh his laugh
its unique chuckle
filled with passion and spark
oh his laugh
lights a spark deep within me

|| **daydreaming** ||

i've kissed you in my dreams
we've danced under the stars
daily, my prayers included your name
my mind created a whole life with you

i've rewritten the script a thousand times
it's all *fictitious thoughts*
like a young schoolgirl

you fit within my world
the melodies we could make
would make music to awaken
what God has hidden in me

|| solid ground ||

tonight is not the night to give in to your fears
to give into your own limitations
stand firm
no need to cry out of desperation
for something you already possess
darling, you have always been loved

|| love matters ||

she's seen too many *tangible* miracles
to not believe God can do one in her love life too

|| give them wings ||

acknowledge the feelings
explore their roots
if the feelings no longer serve you
release them like butterflies
give them permission to spread their wings
and fly

|| holistic ||

people
take a small piece of an aspect of love and call it love
but holistically loving someone is impossible without *christ*

love never fails
love is perfect
God is love

you can only fully receive love
when you have *allowed* love from God

we won't know the full definition of love
until we allow love
to dwell in us

-christ

|| **in the stillness** ||

sometimes you want to sit
in silence with love
absorbing every breath
he graciously gives
inhaling his true essence
exhaling the stresses of the day

|| **crystal clear** ||

she sees the humanity in you
so even when she tries to put you on a pedestal
she's reminded that you are not perfect
and she bends and yields to the movement of your love
extending grace
daily

|| always ||

his love does her heart good
so she vowed to
always keep him close
Jesus

|| always ||

his love does her heart good
so she vowed to
always keep him close
Jesus

|| interested ||

i'm loving the *inner workings* of you
you are exquisite in heart and mind

|| ensemble ||

thinking of you
more than usual
i've allowed God to *resurrect* my heart
his breath sending palpitations
of rhythmic beats and melodies
creating an orchestra of life
flowing through my heart
every day the sounds grow stronger and stronger
preparing me for the day
i allow you into my ensemble

|| love-ethic ||

loving him is far from effortless
loving anyone takes work
the sacrifice of time alone
is enough to make most people throw in the towel
an effortless love does not exist

so i pray my *love ethic*
gets stronger
day by day

|| **concealed** ||

how did i walk past you
day after day
and not notice the *king* in you

175

|| evolving love ||

it was like a slow drip
with every drop
another dose of love
began to drop seeds into the soil of her heart

for once it wasn't an immediate lustful attraction
this was odd in so many ways
she learned that *time* was her friend
she had rushed every aspect of her life

until now
she eased into the evolutionary tale
of two unique people
discovering one another day by day

|| unraveled ||

if i unraveled before you
even in my nakedness
could you still see me as whole

|| engraving ||

i've engraved your handsome face into my memory
i've studied the way your pupils gaze at me
at times intensely and others gently
i've engraved the movement of your lips when you are thinking
and the way they curl up when you chuckle
i've engraved your cologne into my sensory
and the way your masculine hand rests lightly on my knee
what i've engraved the most
is the *peace* of your presence
and the joy God has allowed
us to drink from freely
together

|| kingdom priorities ||

she *dethrones* him daily
because even in all his charm
she knows he is not her savior

|| my knight in shining armor ||

you bring light to my darkness
your glow saturated the charcoal
i've deposited time and time again
dusting me off in your grace
filling me with your love
caressing me in your mercy

|| her future spouse ||

God in his most mysterious ways
whispered to my soul
announcing your arrival
he prepared my mind to not fear
as i await to learn the *art of loving*
and being loved by you

|| jazz vinyl ||

he is like a jazz vinyl
tangible in many ways
he exudes melodies
the keys of my heart
begins to play as he shares
what God is *showing* him
i want to play his record
our conversations
on *repeat*

|| feelings vs peace ||

this *feeling* is too strong
i don't trust it

God's *peace* is too strong
i trust it

|| her sir ||

he knew her story
and *still* pursued her
as if her past was crystal clear

|| she abstains ||

she *refuses* to explore him physically
because she knows
the value of the treasure deep inside of her
is *worth* the wait and commitment

|| artistic love ||

the art in me loves the art in you
when two masterpieces collide
we create a mural with our lives
illuminating the light as it overshadows the valleys

|| her anchor ||

she needs you to be her calm and **not** her storm

her rationale **not** her reason

be her anchor **not** her wind

she needs you to be ***steady***

|| all of you ||

do i still have your attention
even in the midst of the chaos
do your eyes *still search*
tirelessly for mine
waiting to connect
our truths daily

|| all of you ||

do i still have your attention
even in the midst of the chaos
do your eyes *still search*
tirelessly for mine
waiting to connect
our truths daily

|| observations ||

she grew in love at a distance
watching him chase his passions
the *convictions* of his heart led him
to win hers long before he ever said hello

|| **on the limb** ||

how do you know it's real love
how do you know *without* taking the risk
of exploring the unknown of its allure

|| rambunctious girl ||

this time
she gave herself room
to allow space
which gave her *time*
to process
feel
absorb
his energy
and more importantly her own
this momentary pause
brought *clarity*
to her rambunctious heart

|| his ingredients ||

he has the right ingredients
to pour into my being
equipping me to be my best self
to *heal* what's broken
advance what's blooming
reveal what's hidden
he has the right mixture for my soul

|| let's jump ||

let's go all in
off the deep side
into love

partnering to lift up our dreams
as one
pouring hope into our union

allowing love to see us
and *pour his love* through us

|| **his prayers** ||

don't just think about her
pray for her
your thoughts
as thoughtful as they are
don't change her life
but your prayers
elevate her to new heights
gives her a new perspective

|| agape ||

love when it's true
is void of all feelings
powered by *choice*

unwavering
forgiving
surpassing all fear
to unapologetically love

only in the midst of God's presence
can one truly experience *agape*

|| **notions** ||

sensations from our conversations
create an inspiration
igniting my imagination
to paint a configuration
of us in the constellation
of my heart

sensations from our conversations
create an inspiration
igniting my imagination
to paint a configuration
of us in the constellation
of my heart

|| **it's time** ||

cherish the freedom in love
allow it to *blossom*
even in the darkest of nights

|| she who is brave ||

sweetheart
i can't imagine what it took
for you to *stand* at this altar
once again

|| the war ||

she settled the war raging in her heart
she settled in never settling
for anyone *less than* God's best
for her life

leaving behind her own expectations
the laundry list of artificial requirements
ripped them to shreds
the opinions of others are just as irrelevant
as last year's woes

she settled that war raging in her heart
she settled in *only settling*
for the one who matches the description
of God's design for her life and her soul

|| well loved ||

love well
well *beyond your limitations*
love well
well *beyond your fear*
love well
well *beyond your imagination*

|| **love is…** ||

whoever said love is easy
obviously never *sacrificially* loved
another imperfect soul
love requires more than sweet gestures
it's the laying down of yourself
living recklessly selfless
forgiving even when the hurt is still real

allowing one into hidden places
comes with a layer of *vulnerability*
that most don't want to truly feel
opening yourself to another is a sacrifice

sacrificing your security for the exchanges
of oneness with another soul
loving Jesus
loving yourself
and loving your neighbor
is the prerequisite to possessing
a *loved* soul

-Her Loved Soul

About the Author

Briana *Ariel* is a writer, poet, and multidisciplinary artist. Her work encourages women and girls to thrive. Briana Ariel believes the most influential conversation we have throughout our day is the one we have with ourselves. What we speak or secretly believe shapes the viewpoint of our lives. Her message is one of hope, courage, and positive self-talk. Through her words and art, she hopes readers see themselves as strong, beautiful, more than enough, highly capable, and deeply loved.

Briana connects with her readers weekly on her website:
www.BrianaAriel.com

Let's Connect

If you were touched by this book in any way I'd love for you to leave a review, shoot me an email, and share this book with a friend.

www.BrianaAriel.com
Instagram: @ByBrianaAriel

PS: If you read this book, it's not by chance. I prayed for you! Thank you for allowing these words to simmer in your heart.

-Briana Ariel